THE ROYALTY FACTOR
A Writer's Guide to
Reducing Taxes

TAMARA V. BROWN

The Royalty Factor: A Writer's Guide to Reducing Taxes by:
Tamara V. Brown

Published by:
The Insiders Book Club
P.O. Box 507 Hartford, CT 06141
TheInsidersBookClub.com

Copyright © 2016 Tamara V. Brown

ISBN: 978-0-9985152-1-2

DEDICATION

This guide is dedicated to all the writers and authorpreneurs
making it happen!

Table of Contents

ACKNOWLEDGMENTS

Thank you for purchasing The Royalty Factor. I hope you find it helpful. The next addition can only get better with your help.

After reading, please share your feedback by writing a review wherever available, including Goodreads, Amazon, Barnes & Noble, Facebook groups, and personal social media pages.

For more information on publishing, advertising, and small business tax tips, follow:

Periscope: AskTamaraBrown @InsiderBookClub
Instagram: AskTamaraBrown and InsidersBookClub
Twitter: InsiderBookClub
Facebook: InsidersBookClub

You can also visit TheInsidersBookClub.com for a copy of The Royalty Factor Workbook.

INTRODUCTION

The purpose of this book is to build your confidence, as well as help you know the right steps to take in order to reduce your tax liability as a writer or published author. By the end of this book, you will know the correct way to file your income and expenses on your tax return.

Right now, you're not sure if what you've been doing has exposed you to a bigger tax liability. You have expenses, but don't know if they're eligible to claim, or even where to put them on the tax form. You use the software, but that's no help. The questions it asks are confusing, even if it claims to be user-friendly. And going to a tax professional is no better; it can cost you $300 and up to prepare your return. Producing a book is costly enough.

As a writer, I know that the last thing on your mind is the business behind your creativity, especially taxes. It's boring and filled with numbers instead of words. That's why I'm going to make this guide as painless as possible. I'm not going to make this long and drawn out because you've got books to write, not time to waste on taxes.

I'm Tamara V. Brown, a published author and professional tax advisor with over ten years of experience in taxes. Personally, I've filed an income tax as a published author and small-business owner. As a small business owner, every dollar counts. That's why I've learned how to minimize my tax liability as much as possible.

This guide is for writers who receive royalty payments as well as cash for handling their own distribution. I will explain each line that's pertinent to your career as a writer. This is for writers and authors who do not have employees working for them.

It is important that you have an understanding of income tax returns. Even if a professional does your taxes, you should still have an understanding of what's being filed. After all, if it comes down to it, you'll be the one audited, not the person who did it.

The purpose of this book is to show you how to file your income tax, and ways to reduce your liability on that income. The way you reduce your liability is through deductions. The IRS does not care if you claim deductions. They only care about your income. The fewer deductions you claim, the bigger your income. And the bigger the income, the more you're taxed. That's why I want to help you get taxed as little as possible. I will discuss the two ways to report income, as well as walk you through some of the associated forms and schedules.

This book is for information purposes only. I will direct you to several IRS publications that will give your more detailed information.

FAQ

The number one rule when filing your taxes is that you always want to keep your receipts. The IRS can audit you at any time, and they want proof of the numbers written on your tax return. Never think of taxes as a way to earn income; the goal should always be not to owe.

I know this is usually at the end of the book, but in order to help you better understand the anatomy of a tax return, I'm going to start with the FAQ.

What is Income Tax?
Income tax is just what it sounds like: tax on income received. The purpose of filing a return is for the IRS to determine if you paid enough tax on the income you received through the tax year.

If you have an employer, it's more than likely you'll receive a W-2 at the end of the year. The purpose of the W-2 is to show the total income you received, and the amount of federal and state taxes deducted based on that same income (withholdings). If you're a writer, you won't have a W-2 to report your income. Your income will be reported on a 1099-Misc or totaled from transaction receipts without withholdings.

On your return, your total income is calculated to determine your taxable income.

What is Taxable Income?

Taxable income is your true income after adjustments, deductions, and exemptions. When the taxable income amount is determined, a chart determines how much you should be taxed for that year. If you have withholdings from a W-2, or have been paying quarterly taxes throughout the year, you may have already paid the tax determined by your taxable amount. This is how some people get a refund, owe a balance, or break even when filing their income tax. No one is entitled a refund.

Do I Have to File an Income Tax Return?

Whether you have to file a tax return or not is based on total income received throughout the year. Refer to the IRS website's Interactive Tax Assistant (ITA) under "Do I need to file a tax return?" It'll walk you through a series of questions to determine if you need to file a tax return. Before you get started, you'll need to know:
- Your filing status.
- Federal Income tax withheld.
  - If you're an employee, this would be box 2 of the W-2
  - The total amount of estimated taxes paid for the year (refer to the chapter on Estimated Taxes)
- Any information to help you determine your gross income.

Do I Have to Report the Sales of My Book?

If you are required to file an income tax return, yes.

If your only form of income comes from being a writer or published author, you do not have to file a return if your net income was less than $400.

This amount may change, so be sure to check the IRS Self-Employed center under Self-Employed Tax Obligation for changes.

What is Income to a Writer?

Income is the payment you received from writing or selling books.

How is Tax on Income Determined?

The Income Tax form is set up in six sections. Income, Adjusted Gross Income (AGI), Tax and Credits, Other Taxes, Payments, Refund/Balance. Each section flows to the other and is either subtracted or added to the previous amount until you're left with a refund, balance, or have an even balance.

Income - Adjusted Gross Income = Adjusted Gross Income (1040, Line 37)

Adjustment Gross Income - Taxes and Credits = Tax (1040, Line 56)

Tax + Other Taxes = Total Tax (1040, Line 63)

Total Tax - Payments = Refund or Amount You Owe

For the filer, the goal of the income tax form is to make the "Taxable Income" (1040, Line 43) as low as possible.

What is Adjusted Gross Income (AGI)?

The adjusted gross income drives the amount you're taxed, the type, and the amount of credits you receive. To determine the AGI, you subtract the total adjustments from your total income (1040, Line 37 and 38).

Note: Each additional $25 earned is an additional $2-$4 you'll potentially be taxed. Keep this in mind when you think of your net income from your business.

How Do I Classify My Income?

As a writer or published author, it is difficult to classify your income in any way other than a business. Most people write for the purpose of selling their work. In order to do this, you market and promote to an audience of potential customers. To the IRS, you're carrying on tasks with the expectation of making a profit, which are tasks of a business. You may refer to the IRS's 9 Keys to Determine If You're a Business.

Business income is reported on line 12 of the 1040, which is carried over from the schedule C. We will get more into schedule C later in the book.

If you're a writer who is not classified as a business according to the IRS, your income can be reported as a Hobby or Royalty. Both are reported on Line 21 of the 1040.

What is Royalty Income?

To a writer, royalty is money paid to you for the right to use your work. Royalty income is considered Passive income and can be reported as Royalty income on line 21.

What is Hobby Income?

A hobby is something you do for fun with no expectation of making money. It's a hobby if you do it at your leisure and don't expect to make a profit; or have not made a profit.

HOBBY VS BUSINESS

When considering profit, the IRS states that you must be profitable at least three of the last five years to be considered a business. If not, they may classify you as a hobby. If you want to prevent them from changing your classification, you can file a presumption letter (Form 5213). This is a letter asking to postpone the IRS determination in classifying you as a hobby.

Note that it says "profitable," but it does not say how much profit you must have. A profit can be a $5. Make sure you keep this information in mind. Highlight if you must because this will be important later. This will help to determine whether your can claim the income as a hobby or business.

What if I Spent Money?
If you have expenses related to income received as a writer, this is considered a deductible expense. Whether you're reporting income as a hobby or business, you are eligible to deduct expenses.

Deducting expenses is a way to decrease your tax liability. The more income you have, the higher your taxable income. When you deduct expenses from your income, your taxable amount is lowered. The difference between deducting expenses as a business and a hobby is:

- Business expenses are reported on the Schedule C and deducted from the reported gross amount. The net amount is then carried over to the 1040 line 12.
  - Example: If you received $600 in sales, but generated $100 in expenses, the total income reported on your 1040 would be $500 (net amount).
- For Hobby, the gross income amount is reported on the 1040 line 21. However, expenses are reported on Schedule A as a miscellaneous itemized deduction. Hobby expenses are only deductible up to the amount of income received.

Example: If you received $100 as payment for writing, but spent $200 to produce the final product. You can only deduct $100 of your expenses.

Note: You can only deduct the total miscellaneous deduction if it's more than 2% of your AGI. So if your total AGI is $50,000, your total miscellaneous deduction would have to be at least $2000 for it to count as an itemized deduction. So unless you have other miscellaneous deductions, you may not be eligible to claim your hobby expenses.

What is a Standard or Itemized Deduction (1040 Line 40)?
Standard or Itemized deduction is the amount subtracted from your AGI. The subtracted amount is one of the factors in determining your taxable income amount. The higher the deduction, the less you're taxed.

The standard deduction is a flat amount you're eligible for based on your filing status. On the 1040, line 40, there is a box in the left margin that says "Standard Deduction for—." This shows the different standard deduction amount for each filing status.

An itemized deduction (Schedule A) is several different categories added up to determine your deduction amount. In order to use this number, the total must be over the standard deduction amount.

Example: The standard deduction amount for a person with a Single filing status was $6,300 in 2015. In order for a person to itemize, the total deduction claimed on the Schedule A must be over $6,300. If the deduction is $6,301 or more, you are eligible to claim the itemized deduction amount instead of the standard amount.

If the itemized amount is not over the standard deduction amount for your filing status, the standard deduction is automatically used. The categories added up to determine the itemized amount are:

- Medical and Dental Expenses
- Taxes You Paid
- Interest You Paid
- Gifts to Charity
- Casualty and Theft Losses
- Job Expenses and Certain Miscellaneous Deductions
- Other Miscellaneous Deductions

Things you need to know:
- Every category on the Schedule A is NOT 100% deductible. *Refer to the IRS Instructions for Schedule A (Form 1040) to view the limitations. www.irs.gov/schedulea.*
- If your filing status is Married, Filing Separately, you can only claim the itemized deduction if your spouse is claiming an itemized deduction.

SCHEDULE A
(Form 1040)

Department of the Treasury
Internal Revenue Service (99)

Itemized Deductions

OMB No. 1545-0074

▶ Information about Schedule A and its separate instructions is at *www.irs.gov/schedulea*.
▶ Attach to Form 1040.

Name(s) shown on Form 1040 | Your social security number

Medical and Dental Expenses		Caution: Do not include expenses reimbursed or paid by others.		
	1	Medical and dental expenses (see instructions)	1	
	2	Enter amount from Form 1040, line 38 | 2 |		
	3	Multiply line 2 by 10% (0.10). But if either you or your spouse was born before January 2, 1952, multiply line 2 by 7.5% (0.075) instead	3	
	4	Subtract line 3 from line 1. If line 3 is more than line 1, enter -0-		4
Taxes You Paid	5	State and local (check only one box):		
		a ☐ Income taxes, or	5	
		b ☐ General sales taxes		
	6	Real estate taxes (see instructions)	6	
	7	Personal property taxes	7	
	8	Other taxes. List type and amount ▶		
			8	
	9	Add lines 5 through 8		9
Interest You Paid	10	Home mortgage interest and points reported to you on Form 1098	10	
Note: Your mortgage interest deduction may be limited (see instructions).	11	Home mortgage interest not reported to you on Form 1098. If paid to the person from whom you bought the home, see instructions and show that person's name, identifying no., and address ▶		
			11	
	12	Points not reported to you on Form 1098. See instructions for special rules	12	
	13	Mortgage insurance premiums (see instructions)	13	
	14	Investment interest. Attach Form 4952 if required. (See instructions.)	14	
	15	Add lines 10 through 14		15
Gifts to Charity	16	Gifts by cash or check. If you made any gift of $250 or more, see instructions	16	
If you made a gift and got a benefit for it, see instructions.	17	Other than by cash or check. If any gift of $250 or more, see instructions. You **must** attach Form 8283 if over $500 . . .	17	
	18	Carryover from prior year	18	
	19	Add lines 16 through 18		19
Casualty and Theft Losses	20	Casualty or theft loss(es). Attach Form 4684. (See instructions.)		20
Job Expenses and Certain Miscellaneous Deductions	21	Unreimbursed employee expenses—job travel, union dues, job education, etc. Attach Form 2106 or 2106-EZ if required. (See instructions.) ▶	21	
	22	Tax preparation fees	22	
	23	Other expenses—investment, safe deposit box, etc. List type and amount ▶		
			23	
	24	Add lines 21 through 23	24	
	25	Enter amount from Form 1040, line 38 | 25 |		
	26	Multiply line 25 by 2% (0.02)	26	
	27	Subtract line 26 from line 24. If line 26 is more than line 24, enter -0-		27
Other Miscellaneous Deductions	28	Other—from list in instructions. List type and amount ▶		
				28
Total Itemized Deductions	29	Is Form 1040, line 38, over $155,650?		
		☐ **No.** Your deduction is not limited. Add the amounts in the far right column for lines 4 through 28. Also, enter this amount on Form 1040, line 40.	}	29
		☐ **Yes.** Your deduction may be limited. See the Itemized Deductions Worksheet in the instructions to figure the amount to enter.		
	30	If you elect to itemize deductions even though they are less than your standard deduction, check here . . . . ▶ ☐		

For Paperwork Reduction Act Notice, see Form 1040 instructions.   Cat. No. 17145C   Schedule A (Form 1040) 2016

Department of the Treasury – Internal Revenue Service (2016). Schedule A [Itemized Deduction]. Retrieved from https://www.irs.gov/forms-pubs

THE DIFFERENT 1040 FORMS

There are three different tax forms to file your yearly return: 1040 EZ, 1040A, and 1040. No matter how you classify your income, you will always file form 1040. However, I want to let you know the differences for your information only.

1040 EZ
This is the simplest of all the forms because it shows your tax situation is pretty cut and dry.

- Your filing status is either single or married filing jointly
- You don't claim a dependent
- Your taxable income is less than $100,000, and interest is $1,500 or less
- You don't claim adjustments
- You don't itemize
- And you only claim Earned Income Credit

1040A
Like the 1040 EZ, taxable income must be less than $100,000, and you can't itemize when you file form 1040A. However, you can claim certain adjustments. The type of income you can claim is:

- Wages
- Unemployment
- Social Security and Retirement Benefits
- Interest and Dividends
- Pensions, IRAs, and annuities
- Taxable scholarships and grants
- Capital gain distributions

Credits you can claim on the 1040A are:
- Child Tax and Additional Child Tax Credit
- Education credits
- Earned Income Credit
- Child and Dependent Care Expense Credit
- Elderly or disabled credit
- Retirement Savings Contributions Credits

1040

Whatever you can't do on a 1040 EZ and 1040A, you can do on a 1040. This form combines all the information from the schedules you file, including the Schedule C.

FORM 1040 SAMPLE

Form **1040**	Department of the Treasury—Internal Revenue Service (99) **U.S. Individual Income Tax Return**		OMB No. 1545-0074	IRS Use Only—Do not write or staple in this space.

For the year Jan. 1–Dec. 31, 2016, or other tax year beginning _____ , 2016, ending _____ , 20 _____   **See separate instructions.**

Your first name and initial	Last name	Your social security number

If a joint return, spouse's first name and initial	Last name	Spouse's social security number

Home address (number and street). If you have a P.O. box, see instructions.   Apt. no.

▲ Make sure the SSN(s) above and on line 6c are correct.

City, town or post office, state, and ZIP code. If you have a foreign address, also complete spaces below (see instructions).

Presidential Election Campaign
Check here if you, or your spouse if filing jointly, want $3 to go to this fund. Checking a box below will not change your tax or refund. ☐ You ☐ Spouse

Foreign country name	Foreign province/state/county	Foreign postal code

Filing Status
Check only one box.

1. ☐ Single
2. ☐ Married filing jointly (even if only one had income)
3. ☐ Married filing separately. Enter spouse's SSN above and full name here. ▶
4. ☐ Head of household (with qualifying person). (See instructions.) If the qualifying person is a child but not your dependent, enter this child's name here. ▶
5. ☐ Qualifying widow(er) with dependent child

Exemptions

6a ☐ **Yourself.** If someone can claim you as a dependent, **do not** check box 6a . . . . . .
b ☐ **Spouse** . . . .

c **Dependents:** (1) First name Last name	(2) Dependent's social security number	(3) Dependent's relationship to you	(4) ✓ if child under age 17 qualifying for child tax credit (see instructions)
			☐
			☐
			☐
			☐

If more than four dependents, see instructions and check here ▶ ☐

d Total number of exemptions claimed . . . .

Boxes checked on 6a and 6b _____
No. of children on 6c who:
• lived with you _____
• did not live with you due to divorce or separation (see instructions) _____
Dependents on 6c not entered above _____
Add numbers on lines above ▶ ☐

Income

Attach Form(s) W-2 here. Also attach Forms W-2G and 1099-R if tax was withheld.

If you did not get a W-2, see instructions.

7	Wages, salaries, tips, etc. Attach Form(s) W-2	7	
8a	Taxable interest. Attach Schedule B if required	8a	
b	Tax-exempt interest. **Do not** include on line 8a . . .	8b	
9a	Ordinary dividends. Attach Schedule B if required	9a	
b	Qualified dividends	9b	
10	Taxable refunds, credits, or offsets of state and local income taxes	10	
11	Alimony received	11	
12	Business income or (loss). Attach Schedule C or C-EZ	12	
13	Capital gain or (loss). Attach Schedule D if required. If not required, check here ▶ ☐	13	
14	Other gains or (losses). Attach Form 4797	14	
15a	IRA distributions . 15a _____ b Taxable amount . . .	15b	
16a	Pensions and annuities 16a _____ b Taxable amount . . .	16b	
17	Rental real estate, royalties, partnerships, S corporations, trusts, etc. Attach Schedule E	17	
18	Farm income or (loss). Attach Schedule F	18	
19	Unemployment compensation	19	
20a	Social security benefits 20a _____ b Taxable amount . . .	20b	
21	Other income. List type and amount _____	21	
22	Combine the amounts in the far right column for lines 7 through 21. This is your **total income** ▶	22	

Adjusted Gross Income

23	Educator expenses	23	
24	Certain business expenses of reservists, performing artists, and fee-basis government officials. Attach Form 2106 or 2106-EZ	24	
25	Health savings account deduction. Attach Form 8889 . .	25	
26	Moving expenses. Attach Form 3903	26	
27	Deductible part of self-employment tax. Attach Schedule SE .	27	
28	Self-employed SEP, SIMPLE, and qualified plans . .	28	
29	Self-employed health insurance deduction . . .	29	
30	Penalty on early withdrawal of savings	30	
31a	Alimony paid b Recipient's SSN ▶ _____	31a	
32	IRA deduction	32	
33	Student loan interest deduction	33	
34	Tuition and fees. Attach Form 8917	34	
35	Domestic production activities deduction. Attach Form 8903	35	
36	Add lines 23 through 35	36	
37	Subtract line 36 from line 22. This is your **adjusted gross income** . . . . . ▶	37	

For Disclosure, Privacy Act, and Paperwork Reduction Act Notice, see separate instructions.   Cat. No. 11320B   Form **1040** (2016)

Form 1040 (2016) — Page **2**

Tax and Credits	38	Amount from line 37 (adjusted gross income)	38	
	39a	Check if: ☐ You were born before January 2, 1952, ☐ Blind. ☐ Spouse was born before January 2, 1952, ☐ Blind. } Total boxes checked ▶ 39a		
	b	If your spouse itemizes on a separate return or you were a dual-status alien, check here ▶ 39b☐		
Standard Deduction for—	40	Itemized deductions (from Schedule A) or your standard deduction (see left margin)	40	
• People who check any box on line 39a or 39b or who can be claimed as a dependent, see instructions.	41	Subtract line 40 from line 38	41	
	42	Exemptions. If line 38 is $155,650 or less, multiply $4,050 by the number on line 6d. Otherwise, see instructions	42	
	43	Taxable income. Subtract line 42 from line 41. If line 42 is more than line 41, enter -0-	43	
• All others: Single or Married filing separately, $6,300	44	Tax (see instructions). Check if any from: a ☐ Form(s) 8814 b ☐ Form 4972 c ☐	44	
	45	Alternative minimum tax (see instructions). Attach Form 6251	45	
Married filing jointly or Qualifying widow(er), $12,600	46	Excess advance premium tax credit repayment. Attach Form 8962	46	
	47	Add lines 44, 45, and 46 ▶	47	
Head of household, $9,300	48	Foreign tax credit. Attach Form 1116 if required	48	
	49	Credit for child and dependent care expenses. Attach Form 2441	49	
	50	Education credits from Form 8863, line 19	50	
	51	Retirement savings contributions credit. Attach Form 8880	51	
	52	Child tax credit. Attach Schedule 8812, if required	52	
	53	Residential energy credits. Attach Form 5695	53	
	54	Other credits from Form: a ☐ 3800 b ☐ 8801 c ☐	54	
	55	Add lines 48 through 54. These are your **total credits**	55	
	56	Subtract line 55 from line 47. If line 55 is more than line 47, enter -0- ▶	56	
Other Taxes	57	Self-employment tax. Attach Schedule SE	57	
	58	Unreported social security and Medicare tax from Form: a ☐ 4137 b ☐ 8919	58	
	59	Additional tax on IRAs, other qualified retirement plans, etc. Attach Form 5329 if required	59	
	60a	Household employment taxes from Schedule H	60a	
	b	First-time homebuyer credit repayment. Attach Form 5405 if required	60b	
	61	Health care: individual responsibility (see instructions) Full-year coverage ☐	61	
	62	Taxes from: a ☐ Form 8959 b ☐ Form 8960 c ☐ Instructions; enter code(s)	62	
	63	Add lines 56 through 62. This is your **total tax** ▶	63	
Payments	64	Federal income tax withheld from Forms W-2 and 1099	64	
	65	2016 estimated tax payments and amount applied from 2015 return	65	
If you have a qualifying child, attach Schedule EIC.	66a	**Earned income credit (EIC)**	66a	
	b	Nontaxable combat pay election 66b		
	67	Additional child tax credit. Attach Schedule 8812	67	
	68	American opportunity credit from Form 8863, line 8	68	
	69	Net premium tax credit. Attach Form 8962	69	
	70	Amount paid with request for extension to file	70	
	71	Excess social security and tier 1 RRTA tax withheld	71	
	72	Credit for federal tax on fuels. Attach Form 4136	72	
	73	Credits from Form: a ☐ 2439 b ☐ Reserved c ☐ 8885 d ☐	73	
	74	Add lines 64, 65, 66a, and 67 through 73. These are your **total payments** ▶	74	
Refund	75	If line 74 is more than line 63, subtract line 63 from line 74. This is the amount you **overpaid**	75	
	76a	Amount of line 75 you want refunded to you. If Form 8888 is attached, check here ▶	76a	
Direct deposit? See instructions.	b	Routing number ▶ c Type: ☐ Checking ☐ Savings		
	d	Account number		
	77	Amount of line 75 you want applied to your 2017 estimated tax ▶ 77		
Amount You Owe	78	Amount you owe. Subtract line 74 from line 63. For details on how to pay, see instructions ▶	78	
	79	Estimated tax penalty (see instructions)	79	

Third Party Designee — Do you want to allow another person to discuss this return with the IRS (see instructions)? ☐ Yes. Complete below. ☐ No
Designee's name ▶ | Phone no. ▶ | Personal identification number (PIN) ▶

Sign Here — Under penalties of perjury, I declare that I have examined this return and accompanying schedules and statements, and to the best of my knowledge and belief, they are true, correct, and accurately list all amounts and sources of income I received during the tax year. Declaration of preparer (other than taxpayer) is based on all information of which preparer has any knowledge.

Joint return? See instructions. Keep a copy for your records.

Your signature | Date | Your occupation | Daytime phone number
Spouse's signature. If a joint return, **both** must sign. | Date | Spouse's occupation | If the IRS sent you an Identity Protection PIN, enter it here (see inst.)

Paid Preparer Use Only — Print/Type preparer's name | Preparer's signature | Date | Check ☐ if self-employed | PTIN
Firm's name ▶ | | Firm's EIN ▶
Firm's address ▶ | | Phone no.

www.irs.gov/form1040 — Form **1040** (2016)

Department of the Treasury – Internal Revenue Service (2016). 1040 [U.S. Individual Income Tax Return]. Retrieved from https://www.irs.gov/forms-pubs

SCHEDULE C
(BUSINESS INCOME AND DEDUCTIONS)

If you are classified as a business, the Schedule C is where you would report your income and expenses. After deducting your qualified expenses from your income, the net amount will be carried over to the 1040. With the creation of tax software, you just type in the information, and it carries it over to the correct forms and schedules. However, it's important that you understand what's being asked in order to insert the information correctly.

In this section, I will only discuss the lines that are important to you as a writer or published author.

Use this chapter as a guide when sorting your expenses for the tax year. You can also download The Royalty Factor workbook from TheInsidersBookClub.com. When you use the workbook to record your expenses, it tells you which line to carry it over to on the Schedule C.

So let's begin!

Name of Proprietor
Your name.

Box A: Principal business or profession, including product or service

This is the type of business you're are conducting. You can simply put writer or published author.

Box B: Enter code from Instructions

The IRS uses numeric categories to classify your business activities. This helps them determine if you're claiming the correct income and expenseses. Here are the code applicable to writers and authors.

711510 - Independent Artists, Writers, & Performers
511130 - Book Publishers

Box C: Business Name:

This is the registered business name used to obtain your Tax ID. If you are a sole proprietor that has or has not registered, leave it blank.

If you have registered under a "pen name," put down the name used.

Box D: EmployerID number

This is the Tax ID issued to you by the IRS. If you do not have one because you are operating as a sole proprietor, you leave this blank.

Box E: Business Address

Unless you have a physical office, at an address that is not your home, leave this blank.

Box F: Accounting Method

Nine times out of ten, a business in today's world operates as cash.

Box G: Did you "materially participate" in the operation of this business during 2015? If, "No" see instructions for limit on losses

Materially participate means you actively and continually participate in the business of being an writer. You're involved with the promotion, research, and advertising. If you're a writer filling out a schedule C, it is more than likely you matiarlly participate.

Note, if you do not materially particiapate in the operation of the business (passive income), losses are generally not deductible because it's considered royalty income.

Box H: If your started or acquired this business during (current tax year), check here

Check this box if this tax year was the first year you became a published author or paid writer.

Box I: Did you make any payments in (current tax year) that would require you to file Form(s) 1099?

One of the reasons you may have to file a 1099(s) as a writer include paying wages to non-employee(s). This can be a street team you hired to hand out publicity fliers. If you pay a non-employee $600 or more, you must file Form 1099-MISC.

Refer to the IRS General Instructions for Certain Information Returns for further information on 1099(s).

PART I: INCOME

Line 1

This is where you will enter the gross combined income from your business as a writer. If you are an author of multiple published books, you would include the total amount received from all sales. This includes cash receipts and royalty reported on 1099s. If you did speaking engagements for the purpose of increasing your sales, you would include this in your income as well.

It is important that you keep track of the sales you make. One of the things I suggest in my blog titled *Writer's Guide to Events* is a receipt book. When you personally handle sales transactions, you can easily keep track of your sales by using a carbon copy receipt book.

Note: if you receive a royalty on one title, but actively participate in generating income from the other, both would be included in your gross total. Therefore, you would say "Yes" for box G.

Line 2
Unless you sell items that are returnable, this would not apply to you. This is where you would put the total dollar amount that was refunded AFTER a sale. This includes partial refunds.

Note: You cannot count the sales allowance if you did not include the amount in your gross sales. Example: If you sold a book for $10, that amount would be included in the gross sale total on line 1. However, if for some reason, the book was returned, you would also include the $10 on line 2.

Line 3
Cost of Good Sold. This is where you include the cost amount of your inventory. Inventory is an asset you intend to sell at a higher price than what you purchased.

The self-publishing game has changed the way books are distributed. Authors are no longer obligated to print companies who require a minimum print of a few hundred books. Most authors use Print-On-Demand companies where you can print the amount you need instead of having a high number of books you're forced to sell in order to make your money back.

The book industry has also changed with the creation of E-books. This has also eliminated some of the need to have inventory. Instead of shipping physical items, readers can download books with just a click. Therefore, instead of keeping track of inventory, I recommend counting books you purchased as a supply expense and skip this section.

If you're an author who buys a high amount of printed books for the purpose of selling, tracking inventory may be beneficial. To do this, you would need to know the amount on hand at the beginning and end of the tax year. Refer to the IRS section, How to Figure Cost of Goods Sold.

Line 6

If you receive cash for prizes or awards, you will put the total amount for the tax year here.

PART II: EXPENSES

Expenses are any cost incurred in the business of being a writer. Not all expenses are 100% deductible, and some may not be worth claiming. But it's good to keep records and receipts of your expenses because you just never know. I always say, "Better safe than sorry," and "every little bit helps."

Line 8: Advertising

This is any cost you put into marketing and promoting yourself. Here you would include social media promotions, website fees, radio announcements, even vendor fees.

Sometimes it's easy to confuse an advertising cost with the cost of a "supply." The definition of advertising is the act or practice of calling attention to one's product. This is exactly what you want to remember when you think of your advertising expenses. Swag would be an advertising cost, because the purpose is to call attention to your book, website, or service.

Line 9: Car and truck expenses

When you use your vehicle in the everyday operation of your business, some of the expenses are deductible. Car expenses are split between every day and business travel away from the home. "Travel away from the home" means you traveled far enough to need a place to stay. If you don't, this is an ordinary, everyday expense and would be included in this section. If travel was away from the home, keep travel information for line 24a where it can be deducted.

When you deduct vehicle expenses, you have two options: you can either deduct the mileage or the actual expense. This is the same for ordinary travel, and travel away from the home. So you would choose either option for line 9 and line 24a.

Actual expenses includes gas, repairs, insurance, and depreciation of the vehicle. However, actual expenses are limited to the business use only. Unless the vehicle is solely for your use as a writer, your "actual expenses" may be limited.

For example, repairs and maintenance is a necessary expense for the operation of your vehicle. If you only used your vehicle 10% of the time for business, you can only claim up to 10% of the actual expense. However, that 10% is 100% deductible.

For Standard Mileage, you would multiply the number of business miles driven by the cent amount decided by the IRS (it was 57.5 in 2015). You would then add the amount for parking and tolls to get your vehicle expense. Refer to the IRS Standard Mileage Rate for yearly updates.

Example: If you drive 300 business miles and paid $50 in tolls, your standard mileage expense would be $222.50 in 2015. (300 x .575 = 172.50 + 50 = $222.50)

In order to calculate your business miles, record the miles on your odometer before leaving your home, then again when you return home. The difference would be the total business miles driven (as long as you didn't make any casual stops in the middle). It's always good to keep a notepad in your car to keep track of your business miles. You can also record your miles in the Royalty Factor Workbook.

If you lease, you cannot claim actual expenses if you claimed standard expenses the previous year. If you use standard the first year, you must use this method all the years you continue to lease the car.

For more information on Travel, refer to the IRS publication 463, section 4.

Line 11: Contract Labor
Contract labor is a payment to a person (not employee) for a service completed for your business.

For example, if you paid someone a fee to hand out promotional flyers, you would be paying this person as an independent contractor. This also includes fees paid to editors and book cover designers.

The difference between an employee and independent contractor is that you have to withhold certain taxes for employees, where independent contractors, you do not.

Note: If you pay an independent contractor $600 or more, you must file Form 1099-MISC. *Tip:* You can also claim it as an "other expense" on line 27a.expense"

Line 13: Depreciation
Depreciation is an annual deduction allowed in order to recover the cost paid for equipment used beyond the initial year in your business. For example, if you bought a computer the current tax year, the expectation is that you will continue to use the same computer years beyond the initial year you used it for business.

In order to depreciate property, you must be the owner, and it must have a "useful" life of more than one year. If so, every year, as long as it's still working, you can deduct part of the cost on your schedule C.

Depreciation ends when you stop using the property, used all the depreciation, or no longer use the property for business.

In order to depreciate an item, it must be considered a capital asset, such as a computer used in the above example. Other common assets purchased by writers are printing equipment, vehicles*, cell phone*, and exhibitor displays*. If you're a writer with a home office, you can even deduct your office furniture. Refer to the chapter of home office for further details.

You may also be able to depreciate intangible property such a patents or copyrights.

*Refer to The Royalty Factor Workbook for type of exhibitor displays that can be depreciated.

You can only depreciate property up to its useful life (recovery period). A brand new computer is expected to have a usefulness of five years. Therefore, as long as you use that computer for five years, the value is depreciable and eligible to be used as a deduction each year.

Under the IRS, the allowable recovery periods are three years, five years, seven years, ten years, fifteen years, twenty years, and twenty-five years.

Computers, office equipment, cars/trucks, and appliances can be depreciated up to five years. Office furniture and fixtures such as desks can be written off over seven years.

To depreciate property, you need to know:
1. the purchase price (Basis),
2. the date it was put in use for business, and
3. the amount of years you can write off

There are three ways you can depreciate property: Straight-line, Accelerated (MACRS), and Section 179 Deduction.

Straight-Line Method: The property is depreciated an equal amount over the years you can write it off. To determine the total depreciable amount, you have to determine the resell value of the property at the end of its useful life.

Let's use the same computer we bought for $1000. At the end of its useful life, you probably can sell it for about $200. 1000-200 = $800. Divide 800 by 5 and you get a depreciable value of $160 per year.

Accelerated Method: Unlike the straight line, the accelerated lets you take a bigger depreciable value the first year, then smaller deductions later years. To determine the value, you would use the IRS's Modified Accelerated Cost Recovery System (MACRS). Refer to the percentage table guide in the IRS Publication 946.

Section 179: If you want to deduct the entire cost of the property the year it's purchased, you would use this method. However, you are only able to deduct up to the allowable maximum for the year. The allowable maximum is an annual limit set by the IRS.

For more information on depreciation, refer to Publication 946.

Line 15: Insurance
If you have business insurance, you would include your total premium for the year.

Line 16: Interest
If you are claiming a home office expense and pay a mortgage, this is where you include the part of interest covered under your home office. Refer to the chapter on home office for further details.

Line 17: Legal and Professional Services
If you paid an accountant or attorney for an expense directly related to the operation as a writer or published author, include the amount on this line. The services can include paid advice, form preparation, and expenses related to resolving any issue related to your business.

Line 18: Office Expense
An office expense is any necessary supply used in the operation of your business. This includes items like ink, paper, and postage.

Line 20: Rent or Lease

Rent/Lease applies to any vehicle or machine you may have rented or leased during the tax year. For summer events, I've seen authors rent tents and tables if it wasn't included in the vendor fee.

    a.   This line is where you put the amount of any rented vehicle, equipment, or machinery. If you rented a car, make sure you do not also claim this expense under car and truck (line 9) or travel (line 24).

    b.   This line is where you include payments made for renting or leasing office space.

Line 22: Supplies

A supply would be anything purchased for the necessity of your business. The supply has to be used 100 percent for business, and have a useful life of one year or less. Equipment and books bought for research are considered supplies. If the supply has a useful life of over one year, you must deduct it as depreciation and not a supply.

When considering trade show equipment, think about the durability. I bought this silicone sign-up box for events to market my advertising company *The Insiders Book Club*. The intention was to use this box several years because it wasn't used on an everyday basis. However, by the third use it broke apart and can now only be held together with tape. So even if the intention was to depreciate its value, I will count it as a supply because the useful life is less than one year.

If you purchase your own title at wholesale price for resale, it can be considered a supply. Most authors don't order more than necessary, so it's better to count as a supply than inventory. The postage and packaging materials purchased to ship books directly is considered a supply, as well.

Line 23: Taxes and Licenses

If you paid local and state tax for selling books, you would claim it as a deduction in this section. You would only include the gross amount of tax collected.

Note: It is very important that you pay sales tax when required.

Other taxes paid on line 23 that you can include are taxes paid on personal property and real estate, if related to the operation of your business. If you are claiming actual expenses for car and truck, you would claim the same percentage toward paying your local property tax (if applicable). This is the same if you are claiming a home office as an expense.

If you registered as a business with your state, you might be required to pay an annual business entity tax. If you pay this tax to your state, you may include the amount here.

Licenses

This does not apply to all, but some people are licensed with their state as a type of business. I mostly see this with authors who are also publishers. If you are licensed and have to pay an annual fee, you would include the amount on line 23.

Line 24: Travel, Meal, and Entertainment

You can generally benefit from this expense when you travel to book signings, expos, and trade shows. Some expenses related to your trip, meal, lodging, and attendance are deductible.

Before I get into travel, meal, and entertainment, let me first say that this expense is related to yourself only. It does not include your friend, child, or spouse that accompanies you as your "assistant," unless you hired them as a bona fide employee. You can also cover their expense under the pay as an Independent Contractor. However, keep in mind the limitations described under 1099-MISC.

Keep this in mind when you determine whether you'll claim the actual expense or a standard amount. I will get to that part soon.

24a: Travel

In order to claim a travel expense, it must be a necessary expense, meaning you traveled far enough that staying at home was not an option. Your travels must be directly related to business.

Travel Expenses can include:

- Transportation: Airplane, train, bus, or car from your home and business destination.
- Taxi, Commuter Bus, Airport Limousine: between the transportation station and/or lodging to the business location. Note: transportation to or from a business meal may be claimed as an "other expense." See below.
- Baggage and Shipping: Sending baggage, samples, and/or display material from your regular business location to your temporary location. This expense would apply to authors who ship their books and display to hotels when doing signings and expos.
- Car: You can deduct the cost of operating and maintaining your car while away for business. You can also claim business-related tolls and parking.
- Lodging and Meals: If your business trip is overnight or long enough that you have to stop for sleep to properly conduct business. Meals include beverages, taxes, and related tips.
- Cleaning: Dry cleaning and laundry are only included if necessary.
- Telephone: This is for business calls only. It also does not include cell phone expenses that are ordinarily covered by your cell phone carrier, such as local calls. Under telephone, an expense to send a fax can be covered.
- Tips: Any tip you pay under the other covered expenses can be included.
- Other Expense: Any other traveling business expense that is necessary can be included in this section. For example, if

the hotel charges you for WIFI, and the usage is necessary in order to conduct business, this can be covered as an other expense.

If you do not incur any meal expenses, just like vehicle expenses, you can claim a standard amount for incidental instead of the actual cost. Incidentals include tips to baggage carriers, porters, bellhops, hotel maids, stewards/stewardesses, other ship employees and hotel employees in foreign countries.

The incidental-expenses-only method is not subject to the 50% limit discussed below.

You cannot include lodging taxes, telegrams, and cost of telephone calls.

24b: Meals and Entertainment

In most cases, you can only deduct 50% of your actual travel meal and entertainment expense. According to the IRS, *Entertainment includes any activity generally considered to provide entertainment, amusement, or recreation. Examples include entertaining guests at nightclubs; at social, athletic, and sporting clubs; at theaters; at sporting events; on yachts; or on hunting, fishing, vacation, and similar trips.*

Meals could be covered as a form of entertainment if it was provided to a customer or client. For example, if you treated an editor to lunch to discuss the edits to your next book, the meal is deductible.

Entertainment does not include any expense considered leisure, extravagant, amusement, or recreation. Facilities like yachts and hunting cabins are usually not deductible because the primary purpose is entertainment. Meals are only deductible if they are directly related to the conduct of your business.

If you attend conventions and workshops in relation to your business as a writer, you can cover the cost as an entertainment expense if the purpose was to further your trade or business. There must be a scheduled business activities, which is the main reason for the convention. It is a good idea to keep the printed program for your records in the event you are audited.

If the cost of meals is included, the entire thing is considered entertainment.

How to Deduct Meals:

Meals are 50% deductible. If, for any reason, your meal is reimbursed, that amount is NOT deductible. Only the unpaid amount is deductible.

There are two different methods used to deduct meals. You can deduct the actual expense, or deduct a standard amount. The standard amount is a set amount for your daily meals and incidental expenses (M&IE). The standard amount is a federal M&IE rate based on where you traveled.

M&IE rate can be found at www.gas.gov. Click "Per Diem Rates" for locations in and outside the U.S.

If you do no incur any meal expense, or do not use the standard meal allowance, you can claim a standard amount for incidental instead of the actual cost.

For more information on Travel, Entertainment, and Meal deductions, refer to Pub 463.

Line 25: Utilities

If you are claiming a home office expense, you can deduct utilities only up to the percentage used for the business. *Refer to the chapter on business use of the home.*

Telephone:
You can only claim phone usage when the phone is used 100% for business. This includes cell phones. You cannot claim the expense if the phone is also for personal use. If you have a home phone, you

cannot claim the expense unless it is an additional line in your home. If the hook up of the additional line is not located in your home office, you can only deduct the percentage used for business.

Line 27a: Other Expenses
Any expenses not deducted in previous lines would be considered an "other expense." The one thing that comes to mind when it comes to authors is an ISBN.

Note: If you purchase ISBNs in bulk. You can only deduct what was used in the tax year. Example, if you purchased a lot of 10 at $200. Broken down, each cost $20. Therefore, if in the same year, you purchased the ISBN, published the book, and made sales on that same title, the $20 ISBN cost is deductible. If you did the same for 2 books in the same tax year, the total deduction would be $40.

In this chapter, I've walked you through every line that's important to writers and published authors. When you subtract your total expenses from your total income, the amount is carried over to line 12 of the 1040. If you have more expenses than income, you may be able to report the negative amount as a loss. *Refer to the chapter on Net Operating Loss (NOL).*

If you get stuck on anything, refer to the referenced publications.

SCHEDULE C

SCHEDULE C (Form 1040)	**Profit or Loss From Business** (Sole Proprietorship)	OMB No. 1545-0074
Department of the Treasury Internal Revenue Service (99)	▶ Information about Schedule C and its separate instructions is at *www.irs.gov/schedulec*. ▶ Attach to Form 1040, 1040NR, or 1041; partnerships generally must file Form 1065.	

Name of proprietor		Social security number (SSN)

A Principal business or profession, including product or service (see instructions)   **B** Enter code from instructions ▶

C Business name. If no separate business name, leave blank.   **D** Employer ID number (EIN), (see instr.)

E Business address (including suite or room no.) ▶
City, town or post office, state, and ZIP code

F Accounting method: **(1)** ☐ Cash **(2)** ☐ Accrual **(3)** ☐ Other (specify) ▶

G Did you "materially participate" in the operation of this business during 2016? If "No," see instructions for limit on losses . ☐ Yes ☐ No

H If you started or acquired this business during 2016, check here . . . . ▶ ☐

I Did you make any payments in 2016 that would require you to file Form(s) 1099? (see instructions) . . . . . ☐ Yes ☐ No

J If "Yes," did you or will you file required Forms 1099? . . . . ☐ Yes ☐ No

Part I Income

1	Gross receipts or sales. See instructions for line 1 and check the box if this income was reported to you on Form W-2 and the "Statutory employee" box on that form was checked . . . . ▶ ☐	1	
2	Returns and allowances	2	
3	Subtract line 2 from line 1	3	
4	Cost of goods sold (from line 42)	4	
5	**Gross profit.** Subtract line 4 from line 3	5	
6	Other income, including federal and state gasoline or fuel tax credit or refund (see instructions)	6	
7	**Gross income.** Add lines 5 and 6 . . . . ▶	7	

Part II Expenses. Enter expenses for business use of your home **only** on line 30.

8	Advertising	8		18	Office expense (see instructions)	18	
9	Car and truck expenses (see instructions).	9		19	Pension and profit-sharing plans .	19	
10	Commissions and fees .	10		20	Rent or lease (see instructions):		
11	Contract labor (see instructions)	11		a	Vehicles, machinery, and equipment	20a	
12	Depletion	12		b	Other business property . . .	20b	
13	Depreciation and section 179 expense deduction (not included in Part III) (see instructions). . . .	13		21	Repairs and maintenance . . .	21	
				22	Supplies (not included in Part III)	22	
				23	Taxes and licenses	23	
				24	Travel, meals, and entertainment:		
14	Employee benefit programs (other than on line 19). .	14		a	Travel	24a	
15	Insurance (other than health)	15		b	Deductible meals and entertainment (see instructions) .	24b	
16	Interest:			25	Utilities	25	
a	Mortgage (paid to banks, etc.)	16a		26	Wages (less employment credits) .	26	
b	Other	16b		27a	Other expenses (from line 48) .	27a	
17	Legal and professional services	17		b	Reserved for future use . . .	27b	

28	**Total expenses** before expenses for business use of home. Add lines 8 through 27a . . . . . . ▶	28	
29	Tentative profit or (loss). Subtract line 28 from line 7	29	
30	Expenses for business use of your home. Do not report these expenses elsewhere. Attach Form 8829 unless using the simplified method (see instructions). **Simplified method filers only:** enter the total square footage of: (a) your home: _____ and (b) the part of your home used for business: _____. Use the Simplified Method Worksheet in the instructions to figure the amount to enter on line 30	30	
31	**Net profit or (loss).** Subtract line 30 from line 29. • If a profit, enter on both **Form 1040, line 12** (or Form 1040NR, line 13) and on **Schedule SE, line 2.** (If you checked the box on line 1, see instructions). Estates and trusts, enter on **Form 1041, line 3.** • If a loss, you **must** go to line 32.	31	
32	If you have a loss, check the box that describes your investment in this activity (see instructions). • If you checked 32a, enter the loss on both **Form 1040, line 12,** (or Form 1040NR, line 13) and on **Schedule SE, line 2.** (If you checked the box on line 1, see the line 31 instructions). Estates and trusts, enter on **Form 1041, line 3.** • If you checked 32b, you **must** attach **Form 6198.** Your loss may be limited.	32a ☐ All investment is at risk. 32b ☐ Some investment is not at risk.

For Paperwork Reduction Act Notice, see the separate instructions.   Cat. No. 11334P   Schedule C (Form 1040) 2016

Schedule C (Form 1040) 2016   Page **2**

Part III | **Cost of Goods Sold** (see instructions)

33 Method(s) used to
    value closing inventory: **a** ☐ Cost   **b** ☐ Lower of cost or market   **c** ☐ Other (attach explanation)

34 Was there any change in determining quantities, costs, or valuations between opening and closing inventory?
    If "Yes," attach explanation . . . . ☐ Yes   ☐ No

35	Inventory at beginning of year. If different from last year's closing inventory, attach explanation . . .	35
36	Purchases less cost of items withdrawn for personal use	36
37	Cost of labor. Do not include any amounts paid to yourself	37
38	Materials and supplies	38
39	Other costs	39
40	Add lines 35 through 39	40
41	Inventory at end of year	41
42	**Cost of goods sold.** Subtract line 41 from line 40. Enter the result here and on line 4	42

Part IV **Information on Your Vehicle.** Complete this part **only** if you are claiming car or truck expenses on line 9 and are not required to file Form 4562 for this business. See the instructions for line 13 to find out if you must file Form 4562.

43 When did you place your vehicle in service for business purposes? (month, day, year) ▶ ___ / ___ / ___

44 Of the total number of miles you drove your vehicle during 2016, enter the number of miles you used your vehicle for:

a Business _____ **b** Commuting (see instructions) _____ **c** Other _____

45 Was your vehicle available for personal use during off-duty hours? . . . . ☐ Yes   ☐ No

46 Do you (or your spouse) have another vehicle available for personal use? . . . . ☐ Yes   ☐ No

47a Do you have evidence to support your deduction? . . . . ☐ Yes   ☐ No

b If "Yes," is the evidence written? . . . . ☐ Yes   ☐ No

Part V **Other Expenses.** List below business expenses not included on lines 8–26 or line 30.

48	Total other expenses. Enter here and on line 27a	48

Schedule C (Form 1040) 2016

Department of the Treasury – Internal Revenue Service (2016). Schedule C [Profit and Loss from Business]. Retrieved from https://www.irs.gov/forms-pubs

BUSINESS USE OF THE HOME
(FORM 8829, PUB 587)

If you use an area of your home exclusively for business, it may be eligible to be used as a deduction. To be considered a business area, it must be a room or closet. I say closet because if you're a published author who ships books directly to readers, the area used to store your inventory is deductible. In order to claim the use of your home as a deduction, the area must be exclusively used for business, and you must not have any other area outside the home used for business. This does not include the coffee shop down the street.

To claim this deduction, you must know the total square footage of your home, as well as the square footage of the area used as an office or storage.

Just like a vehicle, you can claim the actual expense or use a simplified method. To claim the actual expenses, you will file from 8829 with your schedule C to determine your deductible amount.

Form 8829: Expenses for Business Use of Your Home
To calculate the deductions you have to determine if your expenses are direct or indirect. Direct expenses are expenses related 100% to the business. Indirect are expenses for both the business and personal. Direct and Indirect expenses include:

- Casualty Losses as well as excess
- Mortgage Interest as well as excess
- Real Estate Taxes
- Insurance
- Rent
- Repairs and maintenance
- Utilities
- Depreciation

The percentage of each expense is determined by dividing the square footage used for business by the total area of your home.

Note: there are some situations where you will use less than the determined percentage. For example, electricity. Let's say, according to your calculation, your business space is 25 percent of your total home square footage. However, in your "home office" you only use electricity for lighting at night, and to power up your computer. If you total that up, you may find electricity is usage in your office is only 10 percent of the entire household. Therefore, if your total electricity bill was $100 for the year, you would enter $10 as the direct business expense and nothing in the indirect column.

Simplified Method
Instead of allocating the home expenses, you can choose to use the simplified method. This method is simple as multiplying the area used for business by the flat amount determined by the IRS. In 2015, it was $5. The area claimed cannot be more than 300 square feet.

The good thing about the simplified method is, if used, you can still claim your mortgage interest, real estate taxes, and casualty losses as an itemized deduction on your schedule A. I always tell people, if you're able to itemize, do it!

Things you should know:

- If you have more than one business in your home, the same area cannot be claimed more than once per tax year. This includes someone filing a separate return from you. However, you may divide the shared amount so that each of you could claim a portion.

- If you are claiming a space used to store inventory, it must be the ONLY location used. If you're also storing books at a storage facility down the street, this deduction cannot be used.

- You can go from claiming the actual expenses to the simplified method year to year.

- If you claim the simplified method, all other businesses you're claiming must also use the simplified method. However, the total combined square footage claim cannot be more than 300 square feet.

ESTIMATED TAXES
(FORM 1040-ES)

If you're an employee, federal taxes are usually withheld from your income. The total amount is reflected in box 2 of the company issued W-2. You received your paystub, so you'll see a portion withheld for your federal tax. This is because this tax should be paid as you earn income. As a small business owner, the way to pay your federal income tax is through Estimated Tax. The estimated tax payment you make will also include The Self-Employment Tax.

SELF-EMPLOYMENT TAX

Self-Employment tax (SE tax) is your contribution toward social security and Medicare benefits as a self-employed small business. You must pay SE tax (1040 line 57, Schedule SE) if you have net earnings of $400 or more. (All other requirements do not apply to authors and writers, so I won't go into it.)

You must pay estimated tax if you expect to owe tax of $1,000 or more. This is after you subtract amounts that have already been withheld as an employee, as well as any refundable credits.

To figure your estimated tax amount, you must have a copy of your prior year tax return. Then you would complete the Self-Employment Tax and Deduction Worksheet

You do not need your prior year if:

- The business did not cover all 12 months.
- You had no tax liability or did not have to file a return.

Where Do I Report My Estimated Taxes on the 1040?

Although you pay estimated taxes for your business, you would not report the amount on the Schedule C. The amount you paid would appear on the 1040 line 65.

A full payment of your estimated tax can be made by the income tax file date in April, or you can make four equal payments due April, June, September, and January. (Refer to Form 1040-ES for specific dates and where to send payments)

In the business of being a writer, income changes from year to year. That is why most choose not to make estimated tax payments. Personally, this is why I do not make estimated payments. However, some people are devastated when they find out they owe a balance on their 1040 return. This is why they choose to make estimated tax payments.

Thing you should know:
- If you do not pay estimated taxes, the income tax amount owed will be determined when you file your 1040.

NET OPERATING LOSS (NOL)

When you claim your income as a business (Schedule C), you may have more expenses than income. When this happens, it's called a Net Operating Loss. In most cases, you can claim the loss against your gross income.

Example: You total gross income from your employer and bank interest is $30,000. However, according to the Schedule C, you have a loss of $10,000. Therefore, your reported gross income would be $20,000 instead of $30,000.

Note: If you had a net profit of $10,000 from your business, your gross reported income would be $40,000.

If your loss is more than your total gross income for the year, leaving you with a negative number, on line 41 of the 1040, you may be able to carry the loss over to another year to deduct it from your gross income.

Things you need to know:

- Some losses and carryover are limited.

For more information on NOL, refer to the IRS Publication 536.

FILING ILLUSTRATIONS

The following are examples of how a writer's return may look.

If the form has an X displayed, the box may be applicable to a writer as discussed in this book. However, the X does not apply to this example.

BUSINESS RETURN (SCHEDULE C)

Taxpayer Details:
Single with no dependents
Works from home, but does not claim office use expense
Paid $50 in estimated taxes based on filed 2015 return
No Carry Over losses
Business Registered Under Author Royalty Factor
Employee at XYZ Company with withholding on the W2
Published author registered under the name Royalty Factor earning
$600 in sales.
Claiming the Standard Deduction (does not have enough
deductions to itemize)

SCHEDULE C (Form 1040)	**Profit or Loss From Business** (Sole Proprietorship)	OMB No. 1545-0074
Department of the Treasury Internal Revenue Service (99)	► Information about Schedule C and its separate instructions is at *www.irs.gov/schedulec*. ► Attach to Form 1040, 1040NR, or 1041; partnerships generally must file Form 1065.	Sequence No. 09

Name of proprietor	Social security number (SSN)
YOUR NAME HERE	

A	Principal business or profession, including product or service (see instructions)	B Enter code from instructions
	PUBLISHED AUTHOR	► 7 1 1 5 1 0

C	Business name. If no separate business name, leave blank.	D Employer ID number (EIN), (see instr.)
	AUTHOR ROYALTY FACTOR	S E E B O O K

E	Business address (including suite or room no.) ► N/A
	City, town or post office, state, and ZIP code

F Accounting method: (1) ☑ Cash (2) ☐ Accrual (3) ☐ Other (specify) ►
G Did you "materially participate" in the operation of this business during 2016? If "No," see instructions for limit on losses ☑ Yes ☐ No
H If you started or acquired this business during 2016, check here . . . . ► ☐
I Did you make any payments in 2016 that would require you to file Form(s) 1099? (see instructions) . . . ☐ Yes ☑ No
J If "Yes," did you or will you file required Forms 1099? . . . . ☐ Yes ☐ No

Part I Income

1	Gross receipts or sales. See instructions for line 1 and check the box if this income was reported to you on Form W-2 and the "Statutory employee" box on that form was checked . . . . ► ☐	1	600
2	Returns and allowances	2	
3	Subtract line 2 from line 1	3	
4	Cost of goods sold (from line 42)	4	
5	**Gross profit.** Subtract line 4 from line 3	5	
6	Other income, including federal and state gasoline or fuel tax credit or refund (see instructions) . . .	6	
7	**Gross income.** Add lines 5 and 6 . . . . ►	7	600

Part II Expenses. Enter expenses for business use of your home **only** on line 30.

8	Advertising	8	150	18	Office expense (see instructions)	18	90
9	Car and truck expenses (see instructions)	9	10	19	Pension and profit-sharing plans .	19	
				20	Rent or lease (see instructions):		
10	Commissions and fees .	10		a	Vehicles, machinery, and equipment	20a	50
11	Contract labor (see instructions)	11	20	b	Other business property . . .	20b	
12	Depletion	12		21	Repairs and maintenance . . .	21	
13	Depreciation and section 179 expense deduction (not included in Part III) (see instructions)	13	5	22	Supplies (not included in Part III) .	22	200
				23	Taxes and licenses	23	100
				24	Travel, meals, and entertainment:		
14	Employee benefit programs (other than on line 19) . .	14		a	Travel	24a	200
15	Insurance (other than health) .	15		b	Deductible meals and entertainment (see instructions) .	24b	50
16	Interest:			25	Utilities	25	
a	Mortgage (paid to banks, etc.)	16a		26	Wages (less employment credits) .	26	
b	Other	16b		27a	Other expenses (from line 48) . .	27a	
17	Legal and professional services	17	100	b	**Reserved for future use** . . .	27b	

28	**Total expenses** before expenses for business use of home. Add lines 8 through 27a . . . . . ►	28	975
29	Tentative profit or (loss). Subtract line 28 from line 7	29	

30 Expenses for business use of your home. Do not report these expenses elsewhere. Attach Form 8829 unless using the simplified method (see instructions).
Simplified method filers only: enter the total square footage of: (a) your home: _____
and (b) the part of your home used for business: _____. Use the Simplified
Method Worksheet in the instructions to figure the amount to enter on line 30 . . . . | 30 | |

31	**Net profit or (loss).** Subtract line 30 from line 29.		
	• If a profit, enter on both **Form 1040, line 12** (or **Form 1040NR, line 13**) and on **Schedule SE, line 2.** (If you checked the box on line 1, see instructions). Estates and trusts, enter on **Form 1041, line 3.**	31	-375
	• If a loss, you **must** go to line 32.		

32	If you have a loss, check the box that describes your investment in this activity (see instructions).		
	• If you checked 32a, enter the loss on both **Form 1040, line 12,** (or **Form 1040NR, line 13**) and on **Schedule SE, line 2.** (If you checked the box on line 1, see the line 31 instructions). Estates and trusts, enter on **Form 1041, line 3.**	32a ☑ All investment is at risk.	
	• If you checked 32b, you **must** attach **Form 6198.** Your loss may be limited.	32b ☐ Some investment is not at risk.	

For Paperwork Reduction Act Notice, see the separate instructions.   Cat. No. 11334P   Schedule C (Form 1040) 2016

Form 1040 Department of the Treasury—Internal Revenue Service (99)
U.S. Individual Income Tax Return 2016 OMB No. 1545-0074 IRS Use Only—Do not write or staple in this space.

For the year Jan. 1-Dec. 31, 2016, or other tax year beginning , 2016, ending , 20 | See separate instructions.

Your first name and initial	Last name	Your social security number
FIRST NAME	LAST NAME	X X X X X X X X X

If a joint return, spouse's first name and initial | Last name | Spouse's social security number

Home address (number and street). If you have a P.O. box, see instructions. | Apt. no.
123 ROYAL WAY

▲ Make sure the SSN(s) above and on line 6c are correct.

City, town or post office, state, and ZIP code. If you have a foreign address, also complete spaces below (see instructions).
YOUR CITY, ST, XXXXX

Presidential Election Campaign
Check here if you, or your spouse if filing jointly, want $3 to go to this fund. Checking a box below will not change your tax or refund. ☐ You ☐ Spouse

Foreign country name | Foreign province/state/county | Foreign postal code

Filing Status
Check only one box.

1 ☑ Single
2 ☐ Married filing jointly (even if only one had income)
3 ☐ Married filing separately. Enter spouse's SSN above and full name here. ▶
4 ☐ Head of household (with qualifying person). (See instructions.) If the qualifying person is a child but not your dependent, enter this child's name here. ▶
5 ☐ Qualifying widow(er) with dependent child

Exemptions

6a ☐ **Yourself.** If someone can claim you as a dependent, **do not** check box 6a . . . .
b ☐ **Spouse** . . . .

c Dependents:		(2) Dependent's social security number	(3) Dependent's relationship to you	(4) ✓ if child under age 17 qualifying for child tax credit (see instructions)
(1) First name	Last name			

If more than four dependents, see instructions and check here ▶ ☐

Boxes checked on 6a and 6b: **1**
No. of children on 6c who:
• lived with you
• did not live with you due to divorce or separation (see instructions)
Dependents on 6c not entered above
Add numbers on lines above ▶ **1**

d Total number of exemptions claimed . . . . .

Income

Attach Form(s) W-2 here. Also attach Forms W-2G and 1099-R if tax was withheld.

If you did not get a W-2, see instructions.

7	Wages, salaries, tips, etc. Attach Form(s) W-2	7	50000
8a	Taxable interest. Attach Schedule B if required	8a	
b	Tax-exempt interest. **Do not** include on line 8a . . .	8b		
9a	Ordinary dividends. Attach Schedule B if required	9a	
b	Qualified dividends	9b		
10	Taxable refunds, credits, or offsets of state and local income taxes	10	
11	Alimony received	11	
12	Business income or (loss). Attach Schedule C or C-EZ	12	-375
13	Capital gain or (loss). Attach Schedule D if required. If not required, check here ▶ ☐	13	
14	Other gains or (losses). Attach Form 4797	14	
15a	IRA distributions . 15a	b Taxable amount . . .	15b	
16a	Pensions and annuities 16a	b Taxable amount . . .	16b	
17	Rental real estate, royalties, partnerships, S corporations, trusts, etc. Attach Schedule E	17	
18	Farm income or (loss). Attach Schedule F	18	
19	Unemployment compensation	19	
20a	Social security benefits 20a	b Taxable amount . . .	20b	
21	Other income. List type and amount	21	
22	Combine the amounts in the far right column for lines 7 through 21. This is your **total income** ▶	22	49625

Adjusted Gross Income

23	Educator expenses	23		
24	Certain business expenses of reservists, performing artists, and fee-basis government officials. Attach Form 2106 or 2106-EZ	24		
25	Health savings account deduction. Attach Form 8889 .	25		
26	Moving expenses. Attach Form 3903	26		
27	Deductible part of self-employment tax. Attach Schedule SE .	27		
28	Self-employed SEP, SIMPLE, and qualified plans . .	28		
29	Self-employed health insurance deduction	29		
30	Penalty on early withdrawal of savings	30		
31a	Alimony paid b Recipient's SSN ▶	31a		
32	IRA deduction	32		
33	Student loan interest deduction	33		
34	Tuition and fees. Attach Form 8917	34		
35	Domestic production activities deduction. Attach Form 8903	35		
36	Add lines 23 through 35	36	
37	Subtract line 36 from line 22. This is your **adjusted gross income** . . . ▶	37	49625

For Disclosure, Privacy Act, and Paperwork Reduction Act Notice, see separate instructions. Cat. No. 11320B Form **1040** (2016)

Form 1040 (2016) — Page **2**

Tax and Credits	38	Amount from line 37 (adjusted gross income)		38	49625
	39a	Check if: ☐ You were born before January 2, 1952, ☐ Blind. ☐ Spouse was born before January 2, 1952, ☐ Blind. } Total boxes checked ▶ 39a ☐			
	b	If your spouse itemizes on a separate return or you were a dual-status alien, check here ▶ 39b ☐			
Standard Deduction for— • People who check any box on line 39a or 39b or who can be claimed as a dependent, see instructions. • All others: Single or Married filing separately, $6,300 Married filing jointly or Qualifying widow(er), $12,600 Head of household, $9,300	40	**Itemized deductions** (from Schedule A) or your **standard deduction** (see left margin)		40	6300
	41	Subtract line 40 from line 38		41	
	42	**Exemptions.** If line 38 is $155,650 or less, multiply $4,050 by the number on line 6d. Otherwise, see instructions		42	4050
	43	**Taxable income.** Subtract line 42 from line 41. If line 42 is more than line 41, enter -0-		43	39275
	44	Tax (see instructions). Check if any from: a ☐ Form(s) 8814 b ☐ Form 4972 c ☐		44	5613
	45	Alternative minimum tax (see instructions). Attach Form 6251		45	
	46	Excess advance premium tax credit repayment. Attach Form 8962		46	
	47	Add lines 44, 45, and 46 ▶		47	
	48	Foreign tax credit. Attach Form 1116 if required	48		
	49	Credit for child and dependent care expenses. Attach Form 2441	49		
	50	Education credits from Form 8863, line 19	50		
	51	Retirement savings contributions credit. Attach Form 8880	51		
	52	Child tax credit. Attach Schedule 8812, if required	52		
	53	Residential energy credits. Attach Form 5695	53		
	54	Other credits from Form: a ☐ 3800 b ☐ 8801 c ☐	54		
	55	Add lines 48 through 54. These are your **total credits**		55	
	56	Subtract line 55 from line 47. If line 55 is more than line 47, enter -0- ▶		56	5613
Other Taxes	57	Self-employment tax. Attach Schedule SE		57	X
	58	Unreported social security and Medicare tax from Form: a ☐ 4137 b ☐ 8919		58	
	59	Additional tax on IRAs, other qualified retirement plans, etc. Attach Form 5329 if required		59	
	60a	Household employment taxes from Schedule H		60a	
	b	First-time homebuyer credit repayment. Attach Form 5405 if required		60b	
	61	Health care: individual responsibility (see instructions) Full-year coverage ☐		61	
	62	Taxes from: a ☐ Form 8959 b ☐ Form 8960 c ☐ Instructions; enter code(s)		62	
	63	Add lines 56 through 62. This is your **total tax** ▶		63	5613
Payments If you have a qualifying child, attach Schedule EIC.	64	Federal income tax withheld from Forms W-2 and 1099	64	6000	
	65	2016 estimated tax payments and amount applied from 2015 return	65	50	
	66a	**Earned income credit (EIC)**	66a		
	b	Nontaxable combat pay election	66b		
	67	Additional child tax credit. Attach Schedule 8812	67		
	68	American opportunity credit from Form 8863, line 8	68		
	69	Net premium tax credit. Attach Form 8962	69		
	70	Amount paid with request for extension to file	70		
	71	Excess social security and tier 1 RRTA tax withheld	71		
	72	Credit for federal tax on fuels. Attach Form 4136	72		
	73	Credits from Form: a ☐ 2439 b ☐ Reserved c ☐ 8885 d ☐	73		
	74	Add lines 64, 65, 66a, and 67 through 73. These are your **total payments** ▶		74	6050
Refund Direct deposit? See instructions.	75	If line 74 is more than line 63, subtract line 63 from line 74. This is the amount you **overpaid**		75	437
	76a	Amount of line 75 you want **refunded to you.** If Form 8888 is attached, check here ▶ ☐		76a	
	b	Routing number		c Type: ☐ Checking ☐ Savings	
	d	Account number			
	77	Amount of line 75 you want **applied to your 2017 estimated tax** ▶	77		
Amount You Owe	78	**Amount you owe.** Subtract line 74 from line 63. For details on how to pay, see instructions. ▶		78	
	79	Estimated tax penalty (see instructions)	79	X	
Third Party Designee		Do you want to allow another person to discuss this return with the IRS (see instructions)? ☐ **Yes. Complete below.** ☐ **No** Designee's name ▶ Phone no. ▶ Personal identification number (PIN) ▶			
Sign Here Joint return? See instructions. Keep a copy for your records.		Under penalties of perjury, I declare that I have examined this return and accompanying schedules and statements, and to the best of my knowledge and belief, they are true, correct, and accurately list all amounts and sources of income I received during the tax year. Declaration of preparer (other than taxpayer) is based on all information of which preparer has any knowledge. Your signature / Date / Your occupation / Daytime phone number Spouse's signature. If a joint return, both must sign. / Date / Spouse's occupation / If the IRS sent you an Identity Protection PIN, enter it here (see inst.)			
Paid Preparer Use Only		Print/Type preparer's name / Preparer's signature / Date / Check ☐ if self-employed / PTIN Firm's name ▶ / Firm's EIN ▶ Firm's address ▶ / Phone no.			

www.irs.gov/form1040 — Form **1040** (2016)

As you can see from the example, the writer had more expenses than income, which resulted in a net operating loss. Due to the loss, the filer was able to subtract $375 from the income earned from XYZ Company, making the AGI $49,625. When the deduction(s) and exemption is taken from the AGI, the taxable income is $39,275. This amount is the taxable income we discussed earlier. This amount is used to determine the taxed amount. From the tax table, it's determined this writer's income tax is $5613. (Refer to IRS updates. Exemptions, Deductions, and Tax Table amount changes from year to year)

However, the writer had federal withholdings on the W2 and paid $50 in estimated taxes, which is a total of $6050.

Because the writer paid more taxes than determined by the table, they are entitled to a $437 refund.

HOBBY / ROYALTY RETURN

Taxpayer Details:
Single with no dependents
Employee at XYZ Company with withholdings on the W2
Received 1099 MISC with $600 royalty income
Claiming the Standard Deduction (does not have enough deductions to itemize)

Form **1040**	Department of the Treasury—Internal Revenue Service (99) **U.S. Individual Income Tax Return**		OMB No. 1545-0074	IRS Use Only—Do not write or staple in this space.

For the year Jan. 1–Dec. 31, 2016, or other tax year beginning , 2016, ending , 20 — See separate instructions.

			Your social security number
Your first name and initial	Last name		
FIRST NAME	LAST NAME		X X X X X X X X X
If a joint return, spouse's first name and initial	Last name		Spouse's social security number

Home address (number and street). If you have a P.O. box, see instructions. Apt. no.

123 ROYAL WAY

▲ Make sure the SSN(s) above and on line 6c are correct.

City, town or post office, state, and ZIP code. If you have a foreign address, also complete spaces below (see instructions).

YOUR CITY, ST, XXXXX

Presidential Election Campaign
Check here if you, or your spouse if filing jointly, want $3 to go to this fund. Checking a box below will not change your tax or refund. ☐ You ☐ Spouse

Foreign country name	Foreign province/state/county	Foreign postal code

Filing Status

Check only one box.

1. ☑ Single
2. ☐ Married filing jointly (even if only one had income)
3. ☐ Married filing separately. Enter spouse's SSN above and full name here. ▶
4. ☐ Head of household (with qualifying person). (See instructions.) If the qualifying person is a child but not your dependent, enter this child's name here. ▶
5. ☐ Qualifying widow(er) with dependent child

Exemptions

							Boxes checked on 6a and 6b	1
6a	☐ Yourself. If someone can claim you as a dependent, **do not** check box 6a							
b	☐ Spouse						No. of children on 6c who:	

c	Dependents:	(2) Dependent's social security number	(3) Dependent's relationship to you	(4) ✓ if child under age 17 qualifying for child tax credit (see instructions)
(1) First name Last name				

If more than four dependents, see instructions and check here ▶ ☐

• lived with you
• did not live with you due to divorce or separation (see instructions)

Dependents on 6c not entered above

d	Total number of exemptions claimed			Add numbers on lines above ▶	1

Income

Attach Form(s) W-2 here. Also attach Forms W-2G and 1099-R if tax was withheld.

If you did not get a W-2, see instructions.

7	Wages, salaries, tips, etc. Attach Form(s) W-2	7	50000
8a	Taxable interest. Attach Schedule B if required	8a	
b	Tax-exempt interest. **Do not** include on line 8a	8b	
9a	Ordinary dividends. Attach Schedule B if required	9a	
b	Qualified dividends	9b	
10	Taxable refunds, credits, or offsets of state and local income taxes	10	
11	Alimony received	11	
12	Business income or (loss). Attach Schedule C or C-EZ	12	
13	Capital gain or (loss). Attach Schedule D if required. If not required, check here ▶ ☐	13	
14	Other gains or (losses). Attach Form 4797	14	
15a	IRA distributions 15a b Taxable amount	15b	
16a	Pensions and annuities 16a b Taxable amount	16b	
17	Rental real estate, royalties, partnerships, S corporations, trusts, etc. Attach Schedule E	17	
18	Farm income or (loss). Attach Schedule F	18	
19	Unemployment compensation	19	
20a	Social security benefits 20a b Taxable amount	20b	
21	Other income. List type and amount	21	600
22	Combine the amounts in the far right column for lines 7 through 21. This is your **total income** ▶	22	50600

Adjusted Gross Income

23	Educator expenses	23	
24	Certain business expenses of reservists, performing artists, and fee-basis government officials. Attach Form 2106 or 2106-EZ	24	
25	Health savings account deduction. Attach Form 8889	25	
26	Moving expenses. Attach Form 3903	26	
27	Deductible part of self-employment tax. Attach Schedule SE	27	
28	Self-employed SEP, SIMPLE, and qualified plans	28	
29	Self-employed health insurance deduction	29	
30	Penalty on early withdrawal of savings	30	
31a	Alimony paid b Recipient's SSN ▶	31a	
32	IRA deduction	32	
33	Student loan interest deduction	33	
34	Tuition and fees. Attach Form 8917	34	
35	Domestic production activities deduction. Attach Form 8903	35	
36	Add lines 23 through 35	36	
37	Subtract line 36 from line 22. This is your **adjusted gross income** ▶	37	50600

For Disclosure, Privacy Act, and Paperwork Reduction Act Notice, see separate instructions. Cat. No. 11320B Form **1040** (2016)

Form 1040 (2016)

Page 2

Tax and Credits	38	Amount from line 37 (adjusted gross income)		38	50600
	39a	Check if: ☐ You were born before January 2, 1952, ☐ Blind. ☐ Spouse was born before January 2, 1952, ☐ Blind. } Total boxes checked ► 39a			
	b	If your spouse itemizes on a separate return or you were a dual-status alien, check here ► 39b ☐			
Standard Deduction for —	40	Itemized deductions (from Schedule A) or your standard deduction (see left margin)		40	6300
• People who check any box on line 39a or 39b or who can be claimed as a dependent, see instructions.	41	Subtract line 40 from line 38		41	
	42	Exemptions. If line 38 is $155,650 or less, multiply $4,050 by the number on line 6d. Otherwise, see instructions		42	4050
	43	Taxable income. Subtract line 42 from line 41. If line 42 is more than line 41, enter -0-		43	40250
	44	Tax (see instructions). Check if any from: a ☐ Form(s) 8814 b ☐ Form 4972 c ☐		44	5850
• All others:	45	Alternative minimum tax (see instructions). Attach Form 6251		45	
Single or Married filing separately, $6,300	46	Excess advance premium tax credit repayment. Attach Form 8962		46	
	47	Add lines 44, 45, and 46 ►		47	
Married filing jointly or Qualifying widow(er), $12,600	48	Foreign tax credit. Attach Form 1116 if required	48		
	49	Credit for child and dependent care expenses. Attach Form 2441	49		
	50	Education credits from Form 8863, line 19	50		
Head of household, $9,300	51	Retirement savings contributions credit. Attach Form 8880	51		
	52	Child tax credit. Attach Schedule 8812, if required	52		
	53	Residential energy credits. Attach Form 5695	53		
	54	Other credits from Form: a ☐ 3800 b ☐ 8801 c ☐	54		
	55	Add lines 48 through 54. These are your total credits		55	
	56	Subtract line 55 from line 47. If line 55 is more than line 47, enter -0- ►		56	5850
Other Taxes	57	Self-employment tax. Attach Schedule SE		57	X
	58	Unreported social security and Medicare tax from Form: a ☐ 4137 b ☐ 8919		58	
	59	Additional tax on IRAs, other qualified retirement plans, etc. Attach Form 5329 if required		59	
	60a	Household employment taxes from Schedule H		60a	
	b	First-time homebuyer credit repayment. Attach Form 5405 if required		60b	
	61	Health care: individual responsibility (see instructions) Full-year coverage ☐		61	
	62	Taxes from: a ☐ Form 8959 b ☐ Form 8960 c ☐ Instructions; enter code(s)		62	
	63	Add lines 56 through 62. This is your total tax ►		63	5850
Payments	64	Federal income tax withheld from Forms W-2 and 1099	64	6000	
If you have a qualifying child, attach Schedule EIC.	65	2016 estimated tax payments and amount applied from 2015 return	65	X	
	66a	Earned income credit (EIC)	66a		
	b	Nontaxable combat pay election	66b		
	67	Additional child tax credit. Attach Schedule 8812	67		
	68	American opportunity credit from Form 8863, line 8	68		
	69	Net premium tax credit. Attach Form 8962	69		
	70	Amount paid with request for extension to file	70		
	71	Excess social security and tier 1 RRTA tax withheld	71		
	72	Credit for federal tax on fuels. Attach Form 4136	72		
	73	Credits from Form a ☐ 2439 b ☐ Reserved c ☐ 8885 d ☐	73		
	74	Add lines 64, 65, 66a, and 67 through 73. These are your total payments ►		74	6000
Refund	75	If line 74 is more than line 63, subtract line 63 from line 74. This is the amount you overpaid		75	150
	76a	Amount of line 75 you want refunded to you. If Form 8888 is attached, check here ► ☐		76a	
Direct deposit? See instructions.	b	Routing number	► c Type: ☐ Checking ☐ Savings		
	d	Account number			
	77	Amount of line 75 you want applied to your 2017 estimated tax ► 77			
Amount You Owe	78	Amount you owe. Subtract line 74 from line 63. For details on how to pay, see instructions ►		78	
	79	Estimated tax penalty (see instructions)	79	X	

Third Party Designee

Do you want to allow another person to discuss this return with the IRS (see instructions)? ☐ Yes. Complete below. ☐ No

Designee's name ►	Phone no. ►	Personal identification number (PIN) ►

Sign Here

Under penalties of perjury, I declare that I have examined this return and accompanying schedules and statements, and to the best of my knowledge and belief, they are true, correct, and accurately list all amounts and sources of income I received during the tax year. Declaration of preparer (other than taxpayer) is based on all information of which preparer has any knowledge.

Joint return? See instructions. Keep a copy for your records.

Your signature	Date	Your occupation	Daytime phone number
Spouse's signature. If a joint return, both must sign.	Date	Spouse's occupation	If the IRS sent you an Identity Protection PIN, enter it here (see inst.)

Paid Preparer Use Only

Print/Type preparer's name	Preparer's signature	Date	Check ☐ if self-employed	PTIN
Firm's name ►			Firm's EIN ►	
Firm's address ►			Phone no.	

www.irs.gov/form1040

Form **1040** (2016)

As you can see, because the filer was not able to claim expense deductions, the entire $600 was added to the AGI. Therefore, the refund amount is $150. Less than what it could be if the writer files the income as a business.

THE WRAP UP
MY ADVICE

If taxes were a game, the main objective would be not to owe. When you claim income as a hobby, you can only deduct expenses up to the income. However, not everyone is eligible to use an itemized deduction. Most people who itemize are homeowners with high mortgage interests, or people who pay a high amount in state taxes. So when you think hobby is the way to go, remember you might not be able to claim your eligible deductions. Also, it's hard to prove you're writing as a hobby when the point is to earn income. When you try to earn income, you're acting as a business.

In my opinion, filing as a business is your best option. Remember, I stated earlier that you have to be profitable to be considered a business. However, the IRS does not state how much of a profit. A profit can be $10. This is small enough to increase your tax liability by dollars, if any. So instead of claiming all of your expenses, you may want to consider claiming "just enough." This will prevent you from having to file a presumption letter if you're not profitable for three out of five years. However, if you're only grossing a few dollars a year, filing a hobby is probably beneficial.

Remember to always keep your sale receipts, expense records, and any other document that supports what you're claiming.

Visit TheInsidersBookClub.com to purchase The Royalty Factor workbook to stay organized.

CONCLUSION

It is important that you learn the business mind behind being a creative mind. I hope by now you understand how to reduce your tax liability. You should understand the purpose of filing your income, the basics of a return, and how to report your earnings. Whether you're filing your own 1040, or having it completed by a tax professional, you'll be able to verify the information carried over to the correct lines. Use this guide as a reference while completing your return.

The key rule to business taxes is, keep your receipt for everything. If you need help organizing your expenses, download a copy of The Royalty Factor Workbook. The purpose of the workbook is to categorize your expenses so that you can easily transfer the information when filing your return.

I wrote this book with hopes that it contains everything you need to know about your income tax as a writer. However, it's understandable if you still have questions. I encourage you to follow me @AskTamaraBrown where I give tax tips. You can also schedule a direct consultation where I'll answer any tax question you have.

Visit TheInsidersBookClub.com for other tax tips and to schedule your appointment. You can also download The Royalty Factor workbook.

Regardless, I hope you will contact me after you've filed your return to let me know how painless it was.

Good luck. You got this!

References

Department of the Treasury – Internal Revenue Service (2016). Forms and Publications. Retrieved from https://www.irs.gov

THANK YOU

for purchasing The Royalty Factor

I really appreciate your feedback and would love to know your opinion. The next version can only be better with your help!

Please leave a helpful review on Amazon, Goodreads, Facebook groups, etc..

Thank you!

Tamara Brown
#AskTamaraBrown

ABOUT THE AUTHOR

Tamara inherited her interest in taxes from her mother, who was a certified accountant for thirty years. Her mother would say, "Taxes are something you need to know because they're never going away."

Tamara Brown has since become a certified tax preparer with over ten years' experience in small business. Currently, she is a tax associate for one of the major tax service companies in the U.S. She also provides tax talks to people and organizations around the country.

In addition, she is the founder of *The Insiders Book Club,* which is a direct marketing company for authors, literary businesses, and literary services. She started the company after launching her first fiction novel, *I Keep Holding On.* Like many authors, she felt she would be a best-seller right away. She soon learned it wasn't that easy. At that point, she became determined to learn everything she could about the book industry. By starting The Insiders Book Club, she uses what she learned to help others.